W9-APF-282

A Walk In The Desert

With thanks to Jennifer for all her help—C.A.
For my sons, Matt and Loren—F.T.

Produced by Daniel Weiss Associates, Inc.
33 West 17 Street, New York, NY 10011

Text copyright © 1990 Daniel Weiss Associates, Inc.,
and Al Jarnow

Illustration copyright © Freya Tanz

FIRST FACTS™ is a trademark of Daniel Weiss Associates, Inc.
All rights reserved. No part of this book may be used
or reproduced in any manner whatsoever without written
permission from the publisher.

Published by Silver Press, a division of
Silver Burdett Press, Inc., Simon & Schuster, Inc.
Prentice Hall Bldg., Englewood Cliffs, NJ 07632
For information address: Silver Press.

Printed in the United States of America
10 9 8 7 6 5 4 3 2

Library of Congress Cataloging-in-Publication Data
Arnold, Caroline
A walk in the desert/written by Caroline Arnold;
illustrated by Freya Tanz.
p. cm—(First facts)
Summary: Describes some of the plants and animals that live in
the desert. 1. Desert ecology. [1. Desert ecology. 2. Desert plants.
3. Desert animals. 4. Ecology.] I. Tanz, Freya, ill.
II. Title. III. Series: First facts
Englewood Cliffs, N.J.
QH541.5.D4A76 1990   90-8404
574.5.2652—dc20   CIP
*   AC*
ISBN 0-671-68668-2   ISBN 0-671-68664-X (lib. bdg.)

ISBN 0-382-24649-7 (S/C)

First Facts™

A Walk In The Desert

Written by Caroline Arnold
Illustrated by Freya Tanz

Silver Press

See the bright sun.
Feel the dry air.
It is hot—very hot!
Where are we?

We're in the desert.
Let's take a walk and see what we can find.

The ground is dry in the desert.
It almost never rains.
With so little water,
it is hard for anything to live.
But many plants and animals make their
home in this harsh climate.
You just have to look closely to see them.

Teddy-Bear Cholla Cactus

Barrel Cactus

Hedgehog Cactus

Cactus is one kind of plant
that grows in the desert.
It doesn't have leaves.
Instead, it has sharp spines.
The spines protect the cactus from
animals who might want to eat it.
A cactus stores water in its stem.
It uses the water when there is no rain.

Prickly Pear Cactus

Look up at the tall saguaro.
It is a giant among cactus plants.
It took many years to grow so tall.

In late spring, white flowers bloom.
Birds and insects drink the flowers'
sweet nectar.
After the flowers die, a red fruit grows.

The saguaro cactus is home
to many desert creatures.
Tap, tap, tap, pecks a woodpecker.
It is carving a hole for its nest.
Old holes become nests for other birds.

A hawk is searching for food below.
Its sharp eyes can spot even a tiny mouse.

What is that large bird?
It's a roadrunner.
Coo, coo, coo, it calls.
The roadrunner hardly ever flies,
but it can run fast.
Watch it chase a lizard to eat.

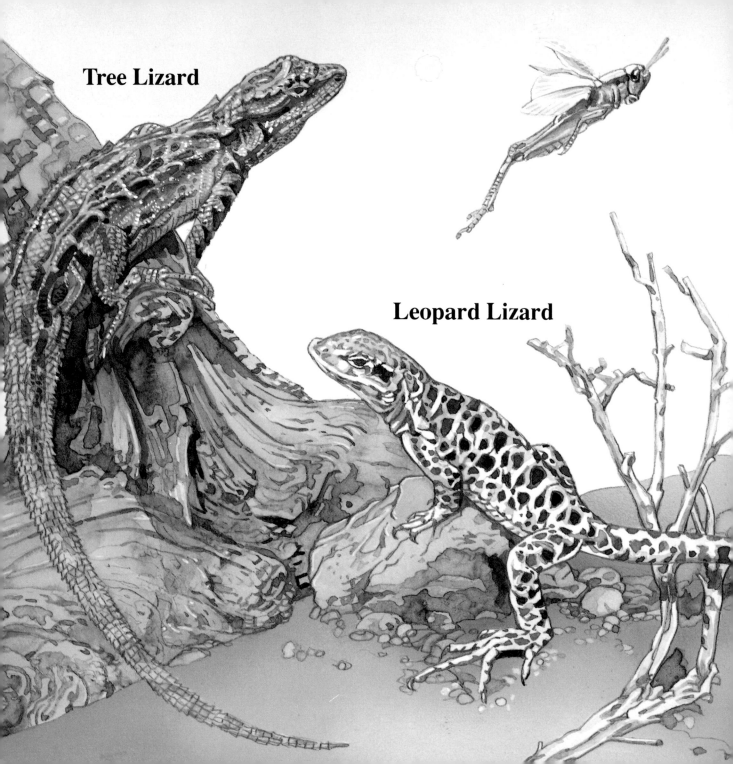

Tree Lizard

Leopard Lizard

Here are some other lizards.
Lizards need the sun's heat
to warm their scaly bodies.
But when it gets too hot,
thcy look for shade.

Zebra-Tailed Lizard

Short-Horned Lizard

A rattlesnake lies next to a rock.
Its earth colors make it hard to see.
Rattlesnakes are dangerous.
A bite from one will kill a small animal.
If you hear a rattlesnake shake its tail,
it is trying to scare you away.

Look! Did you see that rock move?
It isn't a rock at all.
It's a desert tortoise.
The hard shell protects the tortoise
from enemies and from the hot sun.
The tortoise uses its sharp beak
to break off tough desert grasses.
It sometimes eats cactus fruits, too.

The jack rabbit is also a plant eater.
Watch it sniff the early evening air.
It is alert to the sounds and smells
of the desert.
When danger is near, the jack rabbit's long
legs help it to escape quickly.

As night begins to fall,
the desert air cools.
Animals who were hidden or sleeping
come out to hunt and feed.
A hungry coyote howls to the moon.

Do you see the small kit fox?
Big ears help the fox to hear well
so it can track animals to eat.

The cool night is full of activity.

The desert is an exciting place to visit.
You can ride a mule along a deep canyon,

slide down a sand dune,

learn about wildlife at a nature center,
or taste sweet jelly made from prickly pear fruit.

You can find deserts all over the world.
Not all deserts are alike.
Some are hot. Others are cold.
But in all deserts there is little rain.

North
America

South
America

The tiny fennec fox lives
in the world's largest
desert—the Sahara.

The Gila monster
is the only poisonous
lizard in the
American Desert.

Can you find the continent where you live?
Is there a desert on it?

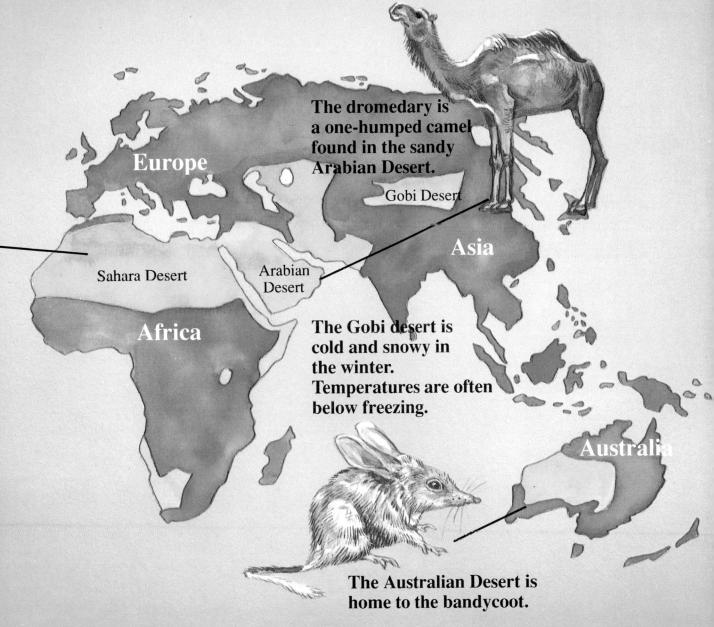

Europe

The dromedary is
a one-humped camel
found in the sandy
Arabian Desert.

Gobi Desert

Asia

Sahara Desert

Arabian
Desert

Africa

The Gobi desert is
cold and snowy in
the winter.
Temperatures are often
below freezing.

Australia

The Australian Desert is
home to the bandycoot.

What did you see on your walk in the desert?
Here are some clues to help you remember.
Can you name each one?